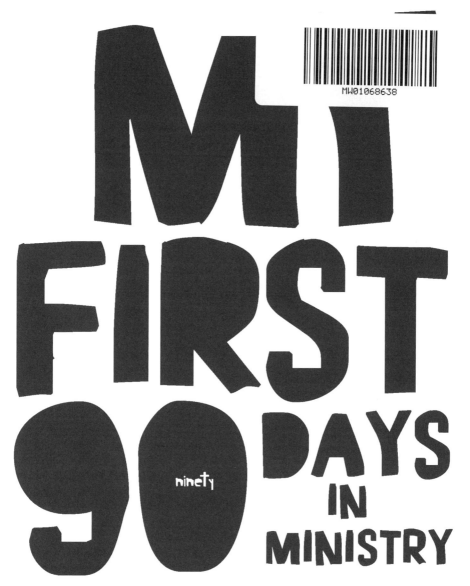

MY FIRST 90 ninety DAYS IN MINISTRY

How to Make a Splash Without Getting All Wet

Group

Loveland, Colorado
group.com

Group resources actually work!

This Group resource incorporates our R.E.A.L. approach to ministry. It reinforces a growing friendship with Jesus, encourages long-term learning, and results in life transformation, because it's

Relational
Learner-to-learner interaction enhances learning and builds Christian friendships.

Experiential
What learners experience through discussion and action sticks with them up to 9 times longer than what they simply hear or read.

Applicable
The aim of Christian education is to equip learners to be both hearers and doers of God's Word.

Learner-based
Learners understand and retain more when the learning process takes into consideration how they learn best.

Incredible things will happen™

Visit our website: **group.com**

Credits
Chief Creative Officer: Joani Schultz
Senior Developer, Children's Ministry: Patty Smith
Senior Editor: Jan Kershner
Senior Project Manager: Pam Clifford
Copy Editor: Julia Wallace
Art Director: Jeff Storm
Interior Designer/Print Production Artist: Cassie Roller and Anne Wilseck
Cover Art Director: Jeff Storm
Illustrator: Cassie Roller
Production Manager: DeAnne Lear

Scripture quotations are taken from the *Holy Bible*, New Living Translation, copyright © 1996, 2004. Used by permission of Tyndale House Publishers, Inc., Carol Stream, Illinois 60188. All rights reserved.

Printed in the United States of America.
10 9 8 7 6 5 4 3 2 1   17 16 15 14 13 12 11 10 09 08

CONTENTS

Introduction

Welcome to the wonderful world of ministry!

No doubt about it—your next three months will be filled with many firsts. We'd like to walk next to you during this exciting time. We'd like to be your partner in ministry and help you make the most of the next 90 days.

Why? We've been "doing ministry" for decades now. We've learned what works and what doesn't. And during that time we've worked closely with many of the movers and shakers in the field. In fact, we've done a bit of moving and shaking ourselves!

This little book contains lots of the pearls we've discovered along the way. Practical tips to help you manage your ministry, balance your life, and navigate the unknown waters on the horizon.

Think of us as your friends. We're on call and ready to help. And think of this book as your ministry primer. Your scrapbook. And the memoir of your first 90 days in ministry.

Congratulations!

Fondly,

Your friends at Group Publishing

one

Your First Day:
Getting Your Feet Wet

OK, this is it.

This is what you've been waiting for, studying for, praying for—your first day on the job!

Excited? You bet.

Nervous? Probably.

Ready to jump in and change the ministry world? Possibly. But first, take time for these three important steps:

1   Find the bathroom.

2   Find the coffee pot.

3   Find a handy place to keep this book. You'll refer to it often during the next 90 days.

All set? Great! Turn the page and let's get started.

Why Are You Here?

Do you remember why you wanted to work in ministry in the first place? Write what you remember about that time—about what prompted you toward ministry.

What were your goals at that time?

What were my first ministry goals and dreams?

Now that I'm ready to begin, what do I hope to accomplish?

What is my definition of a *successful* ministry?

Ideas:

Date:

Is God in Your Goals?

One thing that we've heard from seasoned pastors over the years is the need to keep God in your goals. Without God, you'll accomplish nothing of value. Without God, your work will be in vain.

The key to success? Keep God at the center of your work, your day, your life. Read your Bible. Pray. Then read and pray some more.

Here's how Jim Wideman says it in his book *Children's Ministry Leadership: The You-Can-Do-It Guide,* "Is your heart in tune with God's heart for your ministry? Are you praying? Growing in your relationship with God? Digging into his Word?"

"You can't lead people someplace you've never been. If you want your ministry to grow deeper in the things of the Lord, go there yourself."

> **"Success isn't about how many people attend the service or how much they give. Success is about faithfulness to the call of God on my life, faithfully joining him in what he's doing. Success is about his glory, not mine. Success is about his name, not mine."**
> –David McQueen, *Rev! Magazine's Bathroom Guide to Leadership*

It's time to get started. With God, you can accomplish great things for his kingdom!

> "We now have this light shining in our hearts, but we ourselves are like fragile clay jars containing this great treasure. This makes it clear that our great power is from God, not from ourselves."
> —2 Corinthians 4:7

Take the Plunge: Tips From Seasoned Swimmers

Standing on a diving board, looking down at that expanse of water is kind of like starting your ministry. You're about to plunge into a new environment. It can be a little dizzying, but also exhilarating.

What are three words that describe how you feel right now, as you're ready to take the plunge?

To help you dive gracefully into your new role, we've compiled these practical tips from some of the seasoned swimmers we've worked with over the years.

Find Some Friends

Of anyone in the building, the folks on your church's building maintenance team need to become your best friends—soon.

> They'll be the ones to talk to about painting that ghastly grey wall.
>
> They can help you decide if carpet or tile would be better for the preschool room, and whether you can afford either.
>
> They can help you remove that sagging ceiling tile right over your desk.
>
> These talented people will be worth their weight in gold in your ministry. Buy them coffee. Bring them snacks. Thank them profusely.
>
> And then they can introduce you to your next best friends—the technology team!

In today's world, using technology well can help you excel (it's a joke; get it?) in managing your time, your budget, your goals, your staff—as well as letting you look like a star in your presentations.

Find your techie team and make your introductions. (Coffee and pastries wouldn't hurt, either.)

My First Impression When I Saw My New Office...

Ideas:

Date:

Start Slowly

You're raring to go. Right off the block, you see things you want to change. Things you want to implement. Things you can't wait to try.

Advice from the trenches?

Slow down. Dream big. Start small.

Test the waters.

Get the feel of your job before remodeling the entire ministry.

Get to know your boss...your colleagues.

Get to know your budget.

Be realistic in your expectations.

Dipping Your Toe In...

What do I see as immediate needs in my ministry?

What would I like to accomplish in the next 90 days?

Six months?

One year?

Ideas:

Date:

Once you've assessed the situation and you're ready to begin, consider the following.

Prayer

Make sure that the changes you propose line up with God's plans for your ministry. Pray for guidance.

> **"Instead of making immediate changes, keep a record of all potential changes as soon as you think of them. This allows you to give them prayerful consideration."**
> —Doug Fields, *Your First Two Years in Youth Ministry*

Safety

Your first change, if necessary, should be made in the interest of safety. Depending on your ministry, consider these questions.

- Have you performed background checks on all staff and volunteers? (For more info, see page 24.)

- Do you have a top-notch check-in system for children?

- Do you have adults in the hallways as a "presence"?

- Are your grounds safe? How about your vehicles?

- Do you have all the proper legal forms on hand for your activities?

When it comes to managing your ministry and staff, CVC is *the* organization to join. What's CVC? It's Church Volunteer Central™. A CVC membership offers a wealth of practical wisdom in the form of tips, sample forms, background checks, downloadable art, spiritual gifts assessment, online training, ongoing support—the list goes on and on.

Don't miss out on this valuable tool. Ministry is more fun—*and* more effective—when you're not doing it all yourself. You've got a team that's just waiting to help. For more information, visit ChurchVolunteerCentral.com (or call 1-800-761-2095).

Timing

When is the right time to implement your change? Do you have all the pertinent information you need to make a good decision? Have you checked with the people your change will affect, and gotten their input?

Church Policy

Does your proposed change line up with church policy? With your pastor's vision? Check to make sure.

Hopefully God has called you to ministry for the long haul. So you don't have to change the world right away. It takes time to build a team, build trust, and build a plan.

Caveat: After considering the above, realize that some immediate changes may be necessary. If sound biblical teaching is being compromised, make a change. If it's a matter of safety, make a change. If you face something immoral, make a change.

Otherwise, take it slowly. There's a time for every change you envision.

"For everything there is a season, a time for every activity under heaven."

—Ecclesiastes 3:1

Three
Grab Your Goggles—
You Made the Team!

In the corporate world you hear all kinds of talk about being a team player. Well, it's no different in ministry. Being a team player means that you have the mentality to work well with others, and to commit with others to a common goal. Jesus' disciples were the first ministry team, you know!

But being a member of a team also provides perks that you could never find on your own.

Develop a Dream Team to...Plan

Joani Schultz, Chief Creative Officer at Group Publishing, knows all about dream teams. She developed a children's ministry team at her church.

First, the church announced a meeting open to anyone who was interested in the kids of the church. (Who wouldn't want to attend, right?) She said, "Come dream with us!"

At the meeting, they did just that. What important Bible truths did they want to teach kids? What might that teaching look like? How could they best reach kids?

From that meeting, they developed a core group of volunteers, who in turn funneled into a leadership team. One important component of the final leadership Dream Team was that two people represented each area of children's ministry. No one person was solely responsible for an area or program—there was always a pair. So no one felt alone or overwhelmed.

It was like a ministry buddy system. If scuba divers do it, why can't we? Plus, Jesus sent his disciples out two by two, so the buddy system must work!

The team then got down to the "how to" practical business of developing a children's education program. When it came time to choose a curriculum, the team had already defined its goals—they just had to choose a program that delivered.

For more about how to run your Dream Team meeting, turn to chapter 1 in *Why Nobody Learns Much of Anything at Church: And How To Fix It* by Thom and Joani Schultz.

The Unveiling

After the Dream Team had decided on a new approach to children's education, it was time to unveil their plan to the congregation. Why? Because it was important for the whole church to see how children's ministry fit in with the church doctrine and vision. And it was good for the whole church to know what was going on in the kids' program and to feel good about it. (This approach applies to changes in any ministry area.)

Predictably, Joani had a creative way to announce the Dream Team and the changes they were making. Each duo came forward with a prop that represented their area. The children's Christmas program leaders carried a gift box wrapped in Christmas paper. The nursery leaders carried an actual baby (yes, it belonged to one of the nursery leaders).

You get the picture. It was a fun and memorable way to introduce the team to the congregation. It was a good way for the team to make a positive first impression. It was an affirmation for the team.

And it provided a natural opportunity to invite participation. Joani ended the presentation by saying, "If you want to get connected in children's ministry, we'd love to have you!" Then she gave contact information and arranged convenient entry points into the ministry.

Hint: Never, ever pass up a chance to ask for volunteers! For more on volunteers, check out chapter 5.

"For we are God's masterpiece. He has created us anew in Christ Jesus, so we can do the good things he planned for us long ago."

—Ephesians 2:10

Develop a Dream Team to...Share Responsibility

You have an obligation to work hard in your ministry. But that doesn't mean you need to—or should—work alone.

You can't do it all in ministry. If you try, you'll burn out. It's that simple.

Not only that, but when you *do* burn out, you'll leave a void in your ministry. God's work will suffer. And it will be your doing.

Part of your job is to equip others in the work of the Lord. Doing so faithfully will help you avoid burnout, will allow others to do the work God planned for them, will build ministry ownership, and will make your ministry stronger.

Here are a few tips to help along the way:

Prioritize

God gave you unique talents and skills. Identify them. Use and strengthen them. You've heard it before: What can *only you* do?

> **"It is possible to spread yourself so thin that, within the church, you are mediocre in four or five areas instead of excellent in one or two."**
>
> —Dave Stone, *Keeping Your Head Above Water: Refreshing Insights for Church Leadership*

Delegate

After you've determined what only you can do, find others who can do the things you can't. There are people waiting in the wings who want to help, who can help, who God designed to help. Let them. (But remember to check in regularly with those people. You're still responsible for the tasks you delegate.)

Five People I Still Need to Have Coffee With...

Ideas:

Date:

Manage Your Time

- Write down and evaluate how you spend your time. Too many meetings? (You can do something about that if you're the one calling the meetings. Even if you're not, you may be able to bow out of a few.) Too much time on the phone? (Are all your calls essential? If not, limit them.)

- Is your time gobbled up by e-mails? Designate only one or two times a day to read and respond to e-mails and text messages.

- Get a good day planner. And a good calendar. When you commit a task to paper, you're less liable to get sidetracked.

- Determine when during the day you're most effective. Then use that time for your most challenging tasks.

Develop a Dream Team to...Offer Support

Whether you call them mentors, coaches, or just good friends, you'll need people to turn to for support. In the secular business and health worlds, you can find lots of resources that explain the benefits of having an intentional support system.

But the Bible said it first, of course. Consider Ecclesiastes 4:9-12:

> "Two people are better off than one, for they can help each other succeed. If one person falls, the other can reach out and help. But someone who falls alone is in real trouble. Likewise, two people lying close together can keep each other warm. But how can one be warm alone? A person standing alone can be attacked and defeated, but two can stand back-to-back and conquer. Three are even better, for a triple-braided cord is not easily broken."

Develop your support network. It might include pastors from other churches, your senior pastor, or faithful friends. The key ingredient is that whoever you choose must be willing to be brutally honest with you—and you must be willing to listen.

These relationships can help you through tough times, re-energize you, counsel you, and help you keep your priorities straight. And then you can turn around and help someone else!

Proverbs 27:17

- -

"As iron sharpens iron, so a friend sharpens a friend."

Stop. Think. Write.

My First 30 Days:
What I've Learned So Far...

Ideas:

Date:

Swim Lessons:
The Best Teaching Tools

Once your dream team has helped you formulate a plan for your ministry, it's time to dive in and decide what teaching materials you'll use in your ministry.

Ultimately, it will be your responsibility to choose the resources and to defend your choice, both financially and for content. So you'd better know what to look for in a good curriculum or other teaching tool.

If there's one thing we know here at Group Publishing, it's how to reach and teach people. We've done exhaustive research. We've done more focus groups than we can count. We field test our products and we *know* they work.

So we're confident that if you use one of our resources, your audience will learn. (And you'll look like a genius!) But even if you don't choose one of our products, make sure the teaching tools you choose address the following.

Keep it R.E.A.L.

What's R.E.A.L.? Thought you'd never ask.

Relational.

Learner-to-learner interaction enhances learning and builds Christian friendships. Isn't that what you want from a resource?

Experiential.

What learners experience through discussion and action sticks with them many times longer than what they simply hear or read. When learners experience emotion during an activity, they will automatically remember it—it's how our brains work.

Applicable.

The aim of Christian education is to equip learners to be both hearers and doers of God's Word. Good resources include ways for learners to apply the Bible truths they've learned to everyday life.

Learner-based.

Learners understand and retain more when the learning process takes into consideration how they learn best. Some examples of different learning intelligences, according to Howard Gardner, are visual, linguistic, logical, musical, kinesthetic, intrapersonal, interpersonal, and naturalist. A good curriculum addresses multiple learning styles.

Ask the Right Questions

Make sure that the resources you choose ask effective questions. There are questions, and then there are questions.

Good questions make people in your audience think before they answer. Good questions don't let people slip by with the expected "right" answers. Here are a few tips to help you evaluate the questions in resources.

- Good questions can't be answered with a "yes" or "no."

- Good questions are open-ended.

- Good questions don't have one "right" answer.

- Good questions aren't wordy.

- Good questions involve emotions.

Those are just a few examples of what to look for in a great teaching tool. There are lots of other qualities to be on the lookout for, but we don't have the space to cover them here.

For personal help on the best ways to teach and the best resources to use, take advantage of our Ambassador program. Group has Ambassadors all over the country who lead workshops, help people use Group resources, network with others, and transform lives. There's probably an Ambassador near you! Just call us—remember, we're in this ministry thing together!

Swim Lessons

What are my top 3 priorities in a teaching tool?

Ideas:

Date:

five

Gone Fishin':
Finding Volunteers

Once you've found the perfect resources, the next thing you'll need is people to teach them!

Gathering together a group of qualified volunteers can be a daunting task. In fact, according to our experts, attracting and retaining great volunteers will be an ongoing blip on your sonar screen.

But it can be done! Here are some helpful tips.

Honor the Past

As the new kid in town, you'll inherit a program and its volunteers. No matter what shape that program is in, and no matter how effective the volunteers, honor your predecessor.

There's no need to come in and slam everything and everyone. Keep your opinions to yourself, and slowly make the changes you deem necessary. And it's a good idea, before you make changes, to ask why certain policies and practices are in place. There's plenty you don't know, and there may be a perfectly good reason for that padlock on the supply closet door.

Put Safety First

Make sure—make absolutely sure—that every volunteer and member of your paid staff has gone through a quality background check. Do not skip or procrastinate this step.

The leader in background checks for churches is Church Volunteer Central™. (See page 12). Call them today!

Make It Easy to Serve

More people than you can imagine are ready to serve in your ministry. They just don't know it yet. It's your job to enlighten them. How? Here are some things we've learned over the years.

- Make sure people know your needs. How can people volunteer if they don't know what positions are available?

- Make it easy to step into a role. Some people won't volunteer because they think it will take all of their time. Some don't think they have anything to offer. Let people start small.

> **"Some of the greatest leaders I have known in children's ministry started out in 'easy" positions. Over time, God put a desire in their hearts to do more...Their spiritual gifts blossomed...People who started as greeters became teachers. People who started out passing out papers became small-group leaders."**
> —Dale Hudson, *Turbocharged!*
> *100 Simple Secrets to Successful Children's Ministry*

- Try to match people's spiritual gifts with appropriate positions. Volunteers will be happy to serve when they're using the gifts God gave them. Interview potential volunteers and use a detailed application to assess their strengths.

A Church Volunteer Central™ membership offers, among a ton of other perks, an online spiritual gifts assessment with instant feedback to help volunteers find the perfect spot to serve. (See page 12.)

> **"Their responsibility is to equip God's people to do his work and build up the church, the body of Christ."**
> —Ephesians 4:12

Offer and Expect Commitment

As the leader of your ministry, you need to make certain commitments to your team. Among them, you need to:

- clearly explain expectations;

- offer ongoing training;

- give timely evaluation and feedback;

- foster a sense of unity;

- encourage, praise, and celebrate success; and

- handle problems with integrity and grace.

From your staff, whether paid or volunteer, you have the right to expect commitments to:

- honor a specific term of service,

- openly communicate,

- adhere to the faith tenets of your church, and

- attend training sessions.

Last but Not Least...

Make serving on your team fun! It may not seem important, but it really is.

Bring goodies to meetings. Go for a walk together. Celebrate success. Go overboard in your praise. Have fun as you serve God together!

Matthew 9:38

"So pray to the Lord who is in charge of the harvest; ask him to send more workers into his fields."

Go Fishin'

What am I looking for in a volunteer?

How does my volunteer situation look at the moment?

What do I need to be doing?

Ideas:

Date:

SiX

Be the Strongest Swimmer: Leadership 101

Deciding which resources to use and attracting volunteers to lead them are only two of the many responsibilities you'll be expected to fulfill.

But no matter how many tasks you have to manage, you can tackle them like a true leader!

In no particular order (except for the first few), here are a few prime practices of a great ministry leader.

A great leader in ministry:

Puts Jesus first. Your relationship with Jesus is what your ministry will hinge on. Keep that relationship strong.

> **"Without spiritual health, you won't make it in...ministry. Don't misunderstand: you don't need the knowledge of a Bible scholar or the spiritual disciplines of a monk, but you do need a heart that's tender toward God and open to his leadings. You need to be in love with Jesus."**
> —Doug Fields, *Your First Two Years in Youth Ministry*

Seeks the will of God. As you consider the course you want your ministry to take, consult God. He may have some ideas of his own.

Prays. You're going to be busy, so set aside time to pray. Be deliberate and intentional about your prayer life.

Reads the Bible. Staying in God's Word is essential to a healthy ministry and a healthy life.

> **"Out of the personal reading of God's Word came an inner integrity of witness that had gotten lost in the _doing_ of my ministry. So I urge you...take time with God to allow his Word to refresh your soul, enliven your heart, and strengthen your ministry."**
> —Michael W. Foss, "Tend Your Inner Life,"
> _Dear Pastor: Ministry Advice from Seasoned Pastors_

Listens to the Holy Spirit. God wants to talk to you. He wants to lead you in your ministry. He'll be in touch.

Supports the senior pastor. Show your allegiance to your senior pastor. Don't question senior pastor decisions behind his or her back. Show your support. Keep your senior pastor apprised of your plans. And make sure your ministry vision is in line with that of your senior pastor.

Shares the ministry vision. Don't just share your vision with your core team. Share it with every volunteer. Share it with the entire congregation. Your enthusiasm will be contagious!

Models Christian behavior. Walk the talk. 'Nuff said.

Extends and asks for forgiveness. It's inevitable—you're going to step on some toes along the way. And a few of your own may get crunched, too. Forgiveness is a mending medicine.

Manages money well. If numbers aren't your thing, find someone who loves them. Accurate record keeping helps you stay within your budget and plan effectively.

> **"For I can do everything through Christ, who gives me strength."**
> —Philippians 4:13

Leadership 101

What are my biggest strengths in leadership?

. . . .

. . . .

. . . .

. . . .

What areas do I need to work on?

. . . .

. . . .

. . . .

. . . .

Ideas:

. . . .

. . . .

. . . .

. . . .

. . . .

. . . .

Date:

. . . .

Ready for more? Here are some more characteristics of a great leader.

A great leader:

Disciplines in private. If you wouldn't like to be raked over the coals in public, don't do it to someone else. The Golden Rule still applies.

Praises in public. The opposite of above.

Encourages staff members. Your staff members, both paid and volunteer, need your support. This includes not only training and keeping them in the loop, but regular "atta boys" as well.

> **"I dare you to block out twenty minutes a week simply to encourage your team members! The benefits will astound you."**
> —Dave Stone, *Keeping Your Head Above Water: Refreshing Insights for Church Leadership*

Openly admits mistakes. You're going to make them. Everyone does. Just admit it and move on. (Oh yeah, and try to learn from them.)

Plans ahead. Whether it's next year's Christmas program or next year's budget, don't procrastinate the planning. If you don't know when your church usually orders curriculum or when you need to submit your budget, ask! Ask soon. Don't start out by getting behind.

Brings an agenda to every meeting. A simple thing, yet so important. You'll be surprised how off-track discussions can get if you don't have a plan for your meeting.

Returns phone calls and e-mails. At Group, we have a 24-hour goal of responding to all calls and e-mails, both internal and external. It works well, helps us stay on task, and shows respect for our colleagues and customers.

Never stops learning. Go to conferences that relate to your ministry. Read books on ministry leadership, books that pertain to your specific ministry, and books that will make your job easier along the way (see the reading list at the end of this book). And then network, network, network with other pastors. (Who knows? Maybe you'll write a book someday that will help a rookie pastor!)

Isn't afraid to innovate. Rick Warren, in a Rev! Magazine article titled "Make at Least One Mistake a Week," reminds readers of the faithful risk-taking Jesus related in Matthew 25. It's the story of the three servants who are given a varying amount of talents before their master leaves on a trip. As you know, the master was angry with the servant who risked the least.

Don't be afraid to take risks in your ministry. Pray, do your homework, seek wise counsel—and then take a step of faith if God gives you the green light.

Uses technology to an advantage. Even if you're not technologically savvy, you'll probably want to use audio, video, and computer-based technology in your ministry. So if necessary, start the search right now for someone to help. (Hint: You may find some likely prospects in your church youth group.) You can bet that your audience is used to—and will expect—content to be delivered in an up-to-date manner.

Respects others' time. This goes both for your staff and for the families in your ministry. Take their schedules into account as you plan meetings and events. And if you don't know what times are convenient, ask.

OK, let's take a breath. There are more attributes of great leaders, but that's enough to last you for a few years, right?

And even if you don't possess and can't conjure up all of the leadership qualities above, take heart. God will surround you with capable people to help—people who will exhibit the very qualities you may be low on.

Don't worry. You have God on your side. You have Jesus in your heart. You have the Holy Spirit in your soul.

God wants you to succeed. He has called you to this ministry, and he will be with you every step of the way!

Philippians 1:6

"And I am certain that God, who began the good work within you, will continue his work until it is finally finished on the day when Christ Jesus returns."

Stop. Think. Write.

My First 60 Days:
What I've Learned So Far...

Ideas:

Date:

Seven

Beware of Undercurrents: Resisting Temptation

Let's face it. Jesus was tempted by Satan. Do you really think you're going to get by without being tempted?

Not likely.

In fact, the Bible says we'll be tempted. And it says what to do when it happens—turn to God. Use his strength and his Word. As they say in today's language, the best defense is a good offense. Be ready. Be prepared. Be armed.

> "Put on all of God's armor so that you will be able to stand firm against all strategies of the devil. For we are not fighting against flesh-and-blood enemies, but against evil rulers and authorities of the unseen world, against mighty powers in this dark world, and against evil spirits in the heavenly places.
> "Therefore, put on every piece of God's armor so you will be able to resist the enemy in the time of evil. Then after the battle you will still be standing firm."
> —Ephesians 6:11-13

Unfortunately, we've all read the headlines. Pastors who have fallen into sexual sins, have lied, or who have misappropriated funds. And with every newscast, Christianity takes another knock on the chin.

> "Those who belong to Christ Jesus have nailed the passions and desires of their sinful nature to his cross and crucified them there. Since we are living by the Spirit, let us follow the Spirit's leading in every part of our lives."
> —Galatians 5:24-25

Only you can safeguard your soul. That's between you and God.

But there are a few practical ways to avoid situations that can lead to sin.

In his book *60 Simple Secrets Every Pastor Should Know*, Dave Stone says that he has a window in his office door to protect him from false charges and to prevent him from becoming too casual in conversations with women.

In *Keeping Your Head Above Water: Refreshing Insights for Church Leadership*, Stone also advises watching out for times when you're likely to be vulnerable—times you're lonely, tired, or bored.

He also suggests having an accountability partner, someone you trust and someone who will be completely honest with you. And vice versa.

> **"Several years ago my accountability partner and I made lists of all the people who would be hurt if either of us were to be unfaithful to our wives. It was astounding; it also put the fear of the Lord in us. I encourage every Christian to do this exercise."**
> —Dave Stone, *Keeping Your Head Above Water: Refreshing Insights for Church Leadership*

In *Turbocharged! 100 Simple Secrets to Successful Children's Ministry*, Scott Werner says that men aren't allowed to change diapers in his church nursery. While it may seem sexist, it's a rule his church's insurance carrier insists on.

The Bible says to avoid even the appearance of evil. Be aware and on your guard in one-on-one situations with a member of the opposite sex. You don't have to become paranoid; just careful.

In addition to having a window in your office door or keeping your door ajar during meetings with members of the opposite sex, Stone says in *60 Simple Secrets Every Pastor Should Know*, "Always make certain there is a secretary or another person outside your office if you counsel during off hours. These safeguards can protect you from being tempted and from being falsely accused."

> **"So be careful how you live. Don't live like fools, but like those who are wise. Make the most of every opportunity in these evil days. Don't act thoughtlessly, but understand what the Lord wants you to do."**
> —Ephesians 5:15-17

But sins of a sexual nature aren't the only temptations you may face. In his book *Children's Ministry Leadership: The You-Can-Do-It Guide*, Jim Wideman also mentions the temptation to be lazy, self-sufficient, to compromise on moral issues, and to leave your calling.

The good news is…well…the Good News!

You're not alone. God loves you. He'll help you resist whatever temptation comes your way. It's a promise!

"If you think you are standing strong, be careful not to fall. The temptations in your life are no different from what others experience. And God is faithful. He will not allow the temptation to be more than you can stand. When you are tempted, he will show you a way out so that you can endure."

—1 Corinthians 10:12-13

Beware of Undercurrents

What kinds of temptations am I particularly vulnerable to?

What practical steps can I take to avoid those vulnerable areas?

Ideas:

Date:

eight

Stormy Seas: Solving Problems

It's a part of every job—problem solving.

Problems may come in the form of finances, staff, time management, stress, criticism, or families.

No matter what, though, God will see you through.

> **"Whatever problems you face in ministry, decide to view them not just as problems but also as challenges God wants to help guide you through. That attitude keeps you teachable—and invites God's guidance."**
> —Jim Wideman, *Children's Ministry Leadership: The You-Can-Do-It Guide*

Our seasoned swimmers have all dealt with problems, and have some advice to offer. Here are a few practical tips to help you safely ride those stormy seas.

Deal directly. If you have a problem with someone, go right to that person for a discussion. Don't discuss the problem with anyone else.

Agree to disagree, if necessary. Be aware that you just may not agree with some people, and they may not agree with you. That's OK.

> **"Remember that it's possible to continue a relationship without reaching a resolution. You can walk hand in hand without seeing eye to eye. Or, as we often must say in the church, we don't have to be twins to be brothers."**
> —Rick Rusaw, *60 Simple Secrets Every Pastor Should Know*

Don't take it personally. You're going to deal with difficult people. You're going to get criticism. It comes with the job. Try not to take it personally or dwell on it.

> "A fool is quick-tempered, but a wise person stays calm when insulted."
>
> —Proverbs 12:16

Extend grace. How would Jesus deal with your problem? You bet! He'd be compassionate. He'd forgive. He'd offer grace. And he'd do it without compromising what's right. It's a tough act to follow, but that's what we're called to do.

> **"I know you can deal effectively with difficult people! It's tough, messy, and hard work, but God has called you to love and lead people into a more intimate relationship with him. What a privilege to be used by God—even when it's tough!"**
> —Doug Fields, *Your First Two Years in Youth Ministry*

Manage change. Eventually, you'll want to make a few changes. Probably not this week, but pretty soon, right? Realize that not everyone embraces change. So if you encounter resistance when you try to implement a change, that shouldn't be a surprise. Make sure everyone understands your reasons for the change, and make sure you have all the information you need to support your decision.

Ask for help. It's OK to ask for help and guidance. Really, it is. Ask someone you respect what he or she would do in your situation. Better yet, find someone you respect who's already been in your situation. What worked? What didn't?

Don't put it off. The problem probably isn't going to go away on its own, you know. Might as well deal with it and get it over with.

> **"The most important thing you can do with a problem is also the one thing that may frighten you the most: Confront it head on. Don't ignore it. Don't hope it'll go away or get better on its own. "You're a leader and that means you're a problem solver."**
> —Jim Wideman, *Children's Ministry Leadership: The You-Can-Do-It Guide*
> (**Note:** Jim has a whole chapter on problem solving in this book—it's a great read!)

Pray. Always the best way to deal with any situation.

Trust God. Same as above.

Tough times will come, but with God's help you can handle them!

Psalm 46:10a

"Be still, and know
that I am God!"

Stormy Seas

What types of problems are the most difficult for me to solve? Why?

How do I usually deal with difficult people? How can I improve?

Ideas:

Date:

nine

Staying Afloat: The Fine Art of a Balanced Life

If there's one goal that the seasoned swimmers we've dealt with over the years have agreed on, it's this: try to lead a balanced life.

It's not easy to do that in ministry. You'll have a lot of people making a lot of demands on you. (And one of the most insistent of those people might be you!)

But balance is imperative if you're to accomplish what God has set out for you. You can't be effective if you're exhausted. You can't be effective if you're constantly stressed and overwrought.

But you can do a good job—no, a great job—in your ministry and still remain refreshed in the Lord and available to him and your family.

You can lead a balanced life, even while doing ministry. Here are some tips from the seniors on our swim team.

Keep God first. Keep your priorities straight, and the rest will fall into place. God first—always.

> "And you must love the Lord your God with all your heart, all your soul, and all your strength."
> —Deuteronomy 6:5

Pray. Stay in touch with your Father. He loves you, and has important stuff to say to you.

Plan. We've said it before, but planning ahead will enable you to maintain a reasonable schedule, manage your time, and avoid last-minute dilemmas.

Don't swim solo. You can't do it alone. Don't even try. You'll burn out, and then what good will you be doing?

Rest. The Lord took a day of rest in his week. He tells us to do the same. Take a day off—completely off.

Just say "no." You don't have to take on every task everyone asks of you. It's OK to say "no," especially if doing so will help you to keep your priorities straight.

Cherish your family. The church can find another person to fill your role. Your family can't.

Stay connected to God. Spend time nourishing your own spiritual walk. Take time alone to listen to God, to praise him, and to simply spend time with him.

Don't get discouraged. OK, sometimes you'll get discouraged, but don't let it linger in your mind and heart. Discouragement occasionally comes with the territory—actually it comes with any vocation. When it hits, look to God; he's the source of your strength.

> "Fix your thoughts on what is true, and honorable, and right, and pure, and lovely, and admirable. Think about the things that are excellent and worthy of praise. Keep putting into practice all you learned and received from me—everything you heard from me and saw me doing. Then the God of peace will be with you."
> —Philippians 4:8b-9

Have faith in God, and faith in yourself. God's in control. He put you exactly where you are at this very minute. He called you to this work, to this place and time.

- He will never leave you, never forsake you.

- If you'll let him, God will give you the words to say, the thoughts to think, and the actions to take.

- He knows you can do this—and so do we!

Now get out there and minister!

(P.S.—And stay in touch. Let us know how we can help. You'll find our phone numbers plus an awesome reading list at the back of this book.)

Matthew 28:19-20

"Therefore, go and make disciples of all the nations, baptizing them in the name of the Father and the Son and the Holy Spirit. Teach these new disciples to obey all the commands I have given you. And be sure of this: I am with you always, even to the end of the age."

Staying Afloat: Scriptures to Help

TUESDAY
90

What are my favorite Scriptures?

How can I keep them visible in my ministry?

Ideas:

Date:

Stop. Think. Write.

My First 90 Days:
What I've Learned So Far...

Ideas:

Date:

Ride the Wave: Bonus Handouts

Are your walls still looking a little bare? Well, we have a solution!

Here are some bonus handouts to help you remember what you've learned so far.

Enjoy!

The Top Ten Do's in Problem Solving

10. Do solve the problem—don't run from it.

9. Do solve the problem—don't run from it.

8. Do solve the problem—don't run from it.

7. Do solve the problem—don't run from it.

6. Do solve the problem—don't run from it.

5. Do solve the problem—don't run from it.

4. Do solve the problem—don't run from it.

3. Do solve the problem—don't run from it.

2. Do solve the problem—don't run from it.

1. Do solve the problem—don't run from it.

HOW DOES YOUR CURRICULUM RATE?

Use these questions to analyze the strengths and weaknesses of your present curriculum. Take stock of the teaching methods used. If your curriculum needs improvement, ask what you can do to adapt or replace it.

1. **What seems to be the overall goal of this material?**

   _____ learn historical facts

   _____ learn Bible vocabulary

   _____ emphasize understanding of relevant life principles

   _____ clearly apply Scripture to students' daily lives

2. **What are the tacit objectives?**

   _____ teaching

   _____ cover a lot of material

   _____ keep students busy

   _____ quiet, orderly classroom

   _____ learning

   _____ thorough understanding and retention

   _____ help students think

   _____ active, learning students

3. **Which is most encouraged: lower- or higher-order thinking?**

   _____ fill-in-the-blank exercises

   _____ word games/puzzles

   _____ rote memorization

   _____ closed-ended fact questions

   _____ discovery learning

   _____ thought-provoking activities

   _____ conceptual understanding

   _____ open-ended thinking questions

4. **How is the Bible approached?**

   _____ quotations to be memorized

   _____ stories from history

   _____ glutton approach—the more Bible per lesson the better

   _____ emphasis on biblical detail

   _____ practical truths to be understood

   _____ guidance for students' daily lives

   _____ digestible approach—each lesson provides a nourishing morsel

   _____ emphasis on essential teachings

5. Is the methodology more passive or active?

_____ passive	_____ active
_____ emphasis on receiving information	_____ emphasis on discovering truth
_____ sitting still	_____ moving about
_____ one or two senses involved	_____ several senses involved
_____ teachers lecture	_____ students have conversations
_____ students are the audience	_____ students learn by doing
_____ boring, tedious	_____ fun and/or captivating
_____ teachers tell	_____ teachers ask

6. What are the structures of learning?

_____ individual or competitive	_____ interactive—students work in pairs and small groups
_____ students rely largely on the teacher	_____ students often rely on each other
_____ teachers do all the teaching	_____ students often teach each other
_____ teacher-based	_____ student-based

Responses on the left side of this form indicate less effective learning approaches. Responses on the right side indicate curricular approaches that result in more genuine learning.

Volunteer Evaluation

Date: _____

Your volunteer role: _____

Name (optional): _____

Phone (optional): _____

Please rate your volunteer experience by checking one column for each question:
SD = Strongly Disagree   D = Disagree   A = Agree   SA = Strongly Agree

Fun:
How much fun is it to volunteer at our church?   SD   D   A   SA

1. I tell friends and family about enjoyable things
   that happen to me in my volunteer role at church.

2. I laugh often when I'm volunteering.

3. I enjoy seeing the people I've met through
   my volunteer role.

4. I feel I'm in the right volunteer job.

5. My leaders value me and tell me they value me.

6. I have the training to do my volunteer job
   with excellence.

7. I have the resources to do my volunteer job
   with excellence.

8. I look forward to serving in my volunteer job.

Fair:
In your volunteer role are you treated fairly?   SD   D   A   SA

9. The person who directs me in my volunteer role
   plays favorites among volunteers.

10. The rules I'm expected to obey are clear to me.

	SD	D	A	SA

11. When I fail to meet a job expectation, I receive coaching to help me improve.

12. I'm reviewed regularly and receive insight into how I'm doing in my volunteer role.

13. As a volunteer, my opinion counts.

14. In my volunteer role, I'm treated with respect.

Forgiving:
In your volunteer role are you expected to be perfect—or just growing?

	SD	D	A	SA

15. If I made a mistake that affected the ministry, I'd feel comfortable telling my leader about it.

16. The person who directs me in my volunteer role doesn't talk about other volunteers' mistakes in a harsh way or behind their backs.

17. The person who directs me in my volunteer role has shared with me something he or she did that wasn't successful.

18. In the area in which I volunteer, we have a sense of humor about mistakes that aren't serious.

Faithful:
How much trust do you have in your leaders?

	SD	D	A	SA

19. The person who directs me in my volunteer role cares for me personally.

20. I can talk about requests from my leader and be listened to.

21. The person who directs me in my volunteer role keeps his or her promises.

22. The person who directs me in my volunteer role gives me credit when I do something that's appreciated.

23. The person who directs me in my volunteer role is the sort of person I'd trust to pay me back if he or she borrowed ten dollars.

24. Overall, I am happy with my experience
    as a volunteer.

25. If my circumstances allow it, I will continue to
    volunteer in the future.

26. I believe my leader is following God's direction.

Thank You!

The Next-Level Leader's Prayer

Lord, when I'm serving you and your people, "good enough" just isn't good enough. I want to lead and serve with excellence.

Today give me opportunities to grow in you. I want to become a leader who

- is driven and dedicated.
- knows where I'm going.
- knows where I am.
- has my personal life in order.
- keeps changing my definition of excellence.
- plans ahead—way ahead.
- delegates.
- brings order.
- trains my people.
- connects with other leaders.
- focuses on meeting needs.
- manages people well.
- is a problem solver.
- learns from other leaders.
- doesn't try to do it alone.
- has a shepherd's heart.

Lord, thanks for the privilege of serving. In Jesus' name, amen.

Top Ten List for Mastering Time Management

Here's a quick list of the skills you need to be a certified time management marvel.

10. Account for your time. Do you know how you spent your day? Write it down and evaluate it.

9. Plan your time offensively. Remember: Your time belongs to you. Make a to-do list. Don't automatically say yes when someone asks you for a meeting.

8. Keep your priorities in order. Administer triage with every situation that comes your way. Deal with the big stuff first and the timely stuff first.

7. Delegate to faithful, capable people. What are you doing that someone else could do? Teach someone how to do it, then check in to ensure success.

6. Plan for interruptions. Things won't go exactly as planned; leave room in your schedule to deal with surprises.

5. Respond rather than react to crises. There are always two (or more) sides to a story. Stay calm and get the facts—then make a decision.

4. Don't procrastinate. Don't put off the things you dread.

3. Get help. You don't have all the answers, so find some people who can help you get them. Make a call. Read a book. Seek out a mentor.

2. Plan for growth. People follow a leader who has a plan. What's your plan for growing spiritually, organizationally, and numerically?

1. Pray. Things happen in you and in your ministry when you pray that won't happen any other way.

eleven

Recommended Reading List

Here's a group of books we think could be helpful in the days to come. It's by no means exhaustive, but it's a good place to start.

Happy reading!

Children's Ministry

Children's Ministry in the 21st Century

Take-Out Training for Teachers

Teacher Training on the Go

Turbocharged! 100 Simple Secrets for Successful Children's Ministry

Leadership Essentials for Children's Ministry

Children's Ministry Leadership: The You-Can-Do-It Guide

Lead the Way God Made You

Leadership Essentials for Children's Ministry

Children's Ministry That Works

Volunteers That Stick

Make It R.E.A.L.: Group's Easy Teacher Training & Recruitment

Group's Emergency Response Handbook for Children's Ministry

Children's Ministry Magazine

Youth Ministry

Kurt & Scott's Jr. High Adventure: Taking Your Ministry Beyond Duct Tape, Dodgeball, & Double-Dog Dares

The New Breed: Understanding and Equipping the 21st Century Volunteer

Your First Two Years in Youth Ministry

Group's Emergency Response Handbook for Youth Ministry

Youth Leader Training on the Go

Youth Ministry in the 21st Century

Leaders Are Learners

Youth Ministry in Small Churches

Mentor Me

Group Magazine

Pastor

Why Nobody Learns Much of Anything at Church: And How To Fix It

The Missing Ministry

ME to WE: A Pastor's Discovery of the Power of Partnership

The New Breed: Understanding and Equipping the 21st Century Volunteer

Simply Strategic Stuff: Help for Leaders Drowning in the Details of Running a Church

Simply Strategic Volunteers: Empowering People for Ministry

Simply Strategic Growth: Attracting a Crowd to Your Church

Dear Pastor, Ministry Advice From Seasoned Pastors

The Family-Friendly Church

Keeping Your Head Above Water

60 Simple Secrets Every Pastor Should Know

Rev! Magazine's Bathroom Guide to Leadership

An Unstoppable Force: Daring to Become the Church God Had in Mind

Rev! Magazine

Church Management Resources

Church Volunteer Central

Safe Church

Group Publishing
Please keep in touch with us by calling 1-800-447-1070!

Group's Mission:

We equip churches to help children, youth, and adults grow in their relationship with Jesus.

Volunteers need more than punch and cookies.

Multiplying Ministry From Me to We

Church Volunteer Central®

Invite. Equip. Retain. Lead. Protect.

Get a taste of the good stuff with Church Volunteer Central.
A membership gives you all the ingredients for finding,
growing, and keeping great volunteers.
Expand your ministry. Lighten your load. Calories optional.

Group

Incredible things will happen™

800-761-2095

Start today at www.ChurchVolunteerCentral.com

Dear Group,
Please Make
my Teacher
SAFE For Me.

Thankyou Ethan

Discover...

Kurt & Scott's Junior High Adventure

Taking Your Ministry Beyond Duct Tape, Dodgeball and Double-Dog Dares

by Kurt Johnston & Scott Rubin

Here are practical, on-target tips for moving any junior high ministry beyond duct tape, dodgeball, and double-dog dares. Kurt Johnston and Scott Rubin, junior high pastors at Saddleback Church, tackle how to organize an effective ministry to get the results you want.

ISBN 978-0-7644-3739-7

Discover...

Turbocharged!
100 Simple Secrets to Successful Children's Ministry
by Dale Hudson & Scott Werner

"I can do that!"...is what you'll say after you discover these practical tools and techniques to put your ministry in four-wheel-drive. One hundred high-octane "how-tos" are brought to you by children's ministry leaders who built their ministries from the ground up. They'll show you how to make small changes that gain big results. Plus, they'll share their success stories and ideas for instant tune-ups and major repairs—all in a manual that makes your ministry easier to drive.

ISBN 978-0-7644-3690-1